MW00949520

The Expansion and Apogee of the Ottoman Turkish Empire at the Height of Its Power

By Charles River Editors

A picture of the Ottoman flag

About Charles River Editors

Charles River Editors is a boutique digital publishing company, specializing in bringing history back to life with educational and engaging books on a wide range of topics. Keep up to date with our new and free offerings with this 5 second sign up on our weekly mailing list, and visit Our Kindle Author Page to see other recently published Kindle titles.

We make these books for you and always want to know our readers' opinions, so we encourage you to leave reviews and look forward to publishing new and exciting titles each week.

Introduction

15ᵗʰ century depiction of the Ottoman siege of Constantinople

The Apogee of the Ottoman Empire

In terms of geopolitics, perhaps the most seminal event of the Middle Ages was the successful Ottoman siege of Constantinople in 1453. The city had been an imperial capital as far back as the 4ᵗʰ century, when Constantine the Great shifted the power center of the Roman Empire there, effectively establishing two almost equally powerful halves of antiquity's greatest empire. Constantinople would continue to serve as the capital of the Byzantine Empire even after the Western half of the Roman Empire collapsed in the late 5ᵗʰ century. Naturally, the Ottoman Empire would also use Constantinople as the capital of its empire after their conquest effectively ended the Byzantine Empire, and thanks to its strategic location, it has been a trading center for years and remains one today under the Turkish name of Istanbul.

The end of the Byzantine Empire had a profound effect not only on the Middle East but Europe as well. Constantinople had played a crucial part in the Crusades, and the fall of the Byzantines meant that the Ottomans now shared a border with Europe. The Islamic empire was viewed as a threat by the predominantly Christian continent to their west, and it took little time for different European nations to start clashing with the powerful Turks. In fact, the Ottomans would clash with Russians, Austrians, Venetians, Polish, and more before collapsing as a result of World War I, when they were part of the Central powers.

The Ottoman conquest of Constantinople also played a decisive role in fostering the Renaissance in Western Europe. The Byzantine Empire's influence had helped ensure that it was the custodian of various ancient texts, most notably from the ancient Greeks, and when Constantinople fell, Byzantine refugees flocked west to seek refuge in Europe. Those refugees brought books that helped spark an interest in antiquity that fueled the Italian Renaissance and essentially put an end to the Middle Ages altogether.

In the wake of taking Constantinople, the Ottoman Empire would spend the next few centuries expanding its size, power, and influence, bumping up against Eastern Europe and becoming one of the world's most important geopolitical players. It was a rise that would not truly start to wane until the 19th century. *The Expansion and Apogee of the Ottoman Empire: The History of the Turkish Empire at the Height of Its Power* examines what made the Turks' empire and power grow. Along with pictures of important people, places, and events, you will learn about the apogee of the Ottoman Empire like never before.

Mehmed II

The origins of the Ottoman Empire and the dynasty that founded it are surrounded by legends and mysteries. The mythology around Osman I and his closest family created an image of the dynasty, legitimizing their heritage and right to rule. While some of it surely is true, a lot of it may also be sheer exaggeration. Even the true origin of the Ottoman dynasty is heavily debated by modern historians. The general opinion is that the Ottomans descended from the Kayi tribe, a branch of the Oghuz Turks. This was never mentioned in any records actually written by the time of Osman I's life, but firstly 200 years later, which makes it a highly contested statement. Contemporaneous writers would claim Osman to be a descendant of the Kayi tribe to aggrandize him.

The Kayi Tribe was powerful, prosperous and played an important role in the Caucasus region, both at the time before Osman was born and for hundreds of years to come. To link the Ottoman dynasty with such a tribe would work as an incentive to keep up good relations with the actual Kayi tribe, and also inflate the story about how the Ottoman dynasty descended from power and political influence. It would also support the inherited right of the Ottoman dynasty to rule the area. Though this may never be clearly settled amongst historians today, it is known that Osman's family was one of many Oghuz Turkish people originating from what today is western Kazakhstan, just east of the Caspian Sea.

Osman was the first expansionist chief of what was to be one of the world's greatest empires. After only a few generations, the small *beylik* had grown to include most of Anatolia, the Balkans, and chunks of the Peloponnesus peninsula. By the time of the seventh sultan, Mehmed II, the Ottomans had brought the Byzantine Empire down, formerly the dominant power in the East. This major contestant had been defeated and buried with the conquest of Constantinople in 1453, and the Ottoman Empire had finally displayed its true strength against the Christian alliance in the West. Though Mehmed had already achieved more than many of his predecessors, he did not rest after the conquest. At the end of his reign, he was known all over Europe and Central Asia as the Bloodthirsty, but to his compatriots, he was considered a hero, even to this day. Not only did he annex large portions of territory to his empire, but he also stabilized an area riven by uprisings and political commotion. By developing his militia, the state apparatus, and cultural institutions, he laid the foundation of what would be the apogee of the Ottoman Empire. The inclusion of religious minorities had a positive impact on the prospering empire, and the centuries following are considered a golden age by modern historians.

Mehmed II

After Constantinople had been successfully besieged and conquered, Mehmed claimed the title Caesar—emperor—with the assertion that he was in possession of the former East Roman Empire's capital, as well as having a blood lineage to the former Emperor of the Byzantines by Sultan Orhan I's marriage to a Byzantine princess. The claim was recognised by the Orthodox Church, thanks to the effort made to rebuild and maintain Christian institutions in Constantinople, and the opening of the Ottoman sultanate for both Jewish and Christian minorities.

As an emperor, Mehmed's armies rapidly continued his expeditions to the west. First in line was Serbia, which had long been both a vassal state and an ally of the Ottoman Empire. The two ruling families had intermarried, and the Serbian despot had been by Mehmed and his father's sides in many battles in the previous decades. Mehmed was also married to a family member of the despot, which did not stop the new Serbian king from allying with Hungary, consequently upsetting the Ottoman sultan. It took five years of battles before the Despotate was dissolved, and everything but Belgrade had been ceded to Mehmed. He simultaneously annexed the tip of the Greek peninsula, known as the Despotate of the Morea, to where the Byzantine ex-emperor had fled to live with his brother. Except for a few conclaves belonging to the Venetian Republic, Morea had been dissolved by 1460. It is rumoured that after having conquered the peninsula, upon visiting Troy, Mehmed proudly announced he had avenged the Trojans by ridding the lands of Greek rule.

Mehmed's successes in besieging and annexing new territories seemed perpetual, thanks to his very loyal and competent Grand Vizier Gedik Ahmed Pasha whom, together with governor Turahanoğlu Ömer Bey, led many of the battles on the Balkans and in Greece. While Mehmed was occupied on one front, his officers led fruitful battles all over Eastern Europe, allowing the continuous expansion of Ottoman territory. Leaders of the vassal states tried more than once to rebel against the empire by refusing to pay taxes and forming alliances with Western European kingdoms. Their seditions were more or less futile, and the Ottomans eventually managed to conquer most of the territories they attempted to conquer.

Mehmed led very few losses during his years as a military campaign leader, the most severe of which was in Wallachia, a vassal state of the empire, against the treacherous Vlad III Dracula who, time after time, attacked Turkish forces in the vicinity. After Vlad Dracula had a large number of the Turkish soldiers impaled, Mehmed went to Wallachia to lead a series of battles, eventually ending with an Ottoman victory and a reinstatement of control of the area. At the same time, Mehmed made claims in Moldavia, which turned out to be a costly acquisition to the empire, albeit a victorious one in the end.

Vlad the Impaler

The most serious round of conflicts was the ongoing war against the Republic of Venice. For 16 years, the two powers met in several battles on the Aegean Coast and islands in the Aegean Sea. Venice had dominated the Mediterranean for centuries, and their fleet was outstandingly superior to all other naval powers at the time. During the series of campaigns which became known as the Ottoman-Venetian War, the scales tilted in favor of the Turks. While conquering the island of Lesbos, they also annexed Albania and Negroponte. The war ended with the Treaty of Constantinople in 1479, when the Republic of Venice agreed to cede a few important enclaves on the Dalmatian Coast to the Ottomans in exchange for peace in the ones they were allowed to keep. The treaty also imposed an annual tribute for letting Venice continue to conduct trade in the Black Sea, consequently diminishing their position as a naval trade state in the Levant.

In addition to his focus on the war with the Venetians, Mehmed II also made runs along the Black Sea and sacked the last of the Byzantine successor states, the Empire of Trebizond. Thus, the last vestige of what had been the Roman Empire finally succumbed in 1461. The attack on Trebizond was a pre-emptive strike against a scheming emperor who had been trying to cajole more Christian states to fight the Ottomans and eventually conquer Jerusalem, and these plans gave Mehmed a pretext to erase the last remnants of Byzantium. After the conquest, he allowed the dioceses (administrative areas under the rule of a Christian bishop) to continue administering their services to Christians in the territory.

The Ottoman Empire now had a long stretch of land along the southern coast of the Black Sea, gaining more influence in naval trade. Mehmed took another step toward full dominance when the conditions of the Turkish Tatars living under Genoese rule in the Crimea worsened, and the sultan was called upon for relief. Instead of liberating them, he incorporated the peninsula into the empire, claiming even more of the trade across the Black Sea.

While the war on the Greek Peninsula raged on in irregular bursts, Mehmed was presented with another golden opportunity to conquer an old foe in Anatolia: the Karamanids. After the fall of the Sultanate of Rûm, the Karamanids were the most powerful beylik in Anatolia, but as the Ottoman Empire grew, the Karamanids' influence diminished. At the time of the devastating Battle of Ankara—in which the Central Asian ruler, Timur, crushed the Ottoman armies and killed the sultan—Anatolia fell into disarray. The Karamanids made some effort to re-establish themselves as Anatolia's ruling power, but after the Ottoman Interregnum ended a decade later, the claimed lands were quickly taken back. The antagonism between the Ottoman dynasty and the Karamanids kept rising to the surface over the centuries. When the tables had turned and civil war had broken out amongst Karamanid heirs, Mehmed simply walked in to annex the territory. After another decade, he decided to completely subsume the Karamanid state, abolishing it. In doing so, he also displaced the entire population to the enclaves around his empire to prevent them from uniting and rising against the Ottomans again.

At the end of Mehmed's reign, it was clear that he had been the most important leader of the Ottoman Empire up to that point, except for the founder himself. Apart from the territorial gains, he made significant changes to how the empire was administered. With him, the practice of devshirme was perfected, while the Janissaries gained importance and reliably supported the sultan. To establish complete loyalty and trust between Mehmed and his viziers—whose responsibilities and autonomy steadily grew—Mehmed recruited them via the devshirme rather than from the usual noble families. By elevating poorer families' status and economic stability, he gained the trust of subjects who, by his choosing, would become high-earning officers and members of the government. He also systematically registered his chief officials, created records of their titles, salaries, and responsibilities, and how they were related to each other and the sultan. He broke with the Ghazi tradition of ceremonies and rituals where certain people held a higher rank depending on their heritage. He also gave payment to religious scholars, making them loyal to him and subsequently coming to his defence in religious matters associated with his authoritarian rule. His most important contribution was the institution of a secular code of law in matters where Sharia law couldn't be used. These laws, called kanunnames, dealt mainly with economic and fiscal matters, shedding a pragmatic light on administrative questions arising around the empire. At the same time as Mehmed distributed the power of the empire to more and stronger viziers, he also consolidated his power as the autonomous ruler, excluding himself from the lower officials, so the people had no access to him. His viziers and administrative employees dealt with questions arising on the ground, while he made authoritarian decisions about the structure and build of the empire. Not surprisingly, it was Mehmed who had introduced the word "politics" to the Ottoman Empire.

That said, not everything was politics under Mehmed II's rule. He was apt when it came to cultural and religious matters and entertained scholars, artists, poets, and theologians from the East and West. His court was a multicultural mix of science, religion, and art, where Italian painters, Christian patriarchs, and Persian poets intermingled. He encouraged the translation of the Christian doctrine into Turkish to better understand the minority groups in his empire, and he eventually established the first version of the millets, autonomous courts of laws where Jews, Christians, and Muslims could be tried according to a separate legislature of their religious laws. This let people practice their religion freely within the Ottoman domain, more or less ruling themselves in personal matters without interference from the Ottoman government. The millets came to full practice with the extended and more intricate upgrade of the Kanunnames under the rule of Mehmed's grandson, Suleiman.

Mehmed's final quest was an attempt to conquer Italy. In Rome, the Pope feared suffering the same fate Constantinople did, so he rallied other Christian states to come to his aid. The Republic of Venice was the only one to refuse out of respect for the peace treaty they had signed with the Ottomans in 1479. Hungary, France, and several other of the Italian city-states replied to the appeal, and in the end, the Ottoman expedition in Italy was short-lived. After conquering Otranto in 1480, they negotiated to give it back to Rome in exchange for free passage while withdrawing from Italy.

Mehmed died shortly after this endeavour under mysterious circumstances. Out campaigning, showing no signs of weakness or disease, he suddenly fell seriously ill and died within a few days. Some historians claim Mehmed's son and heir, Bayezid II, had poisoned him, while others say it was due to old age and natural causes. Mehmed was in the midst of planning a possible takeover in Egypt when he died, a dream which did not materialize, much to the joy of the Mamluks ruling the southern Mediterranean coast.

At the news of Mehmed's death, church bells rang throughout Europe, and the Western kings expressed hope of enjoying a respite from Ottoman aggression. Bayezid took the throne, and in accordance with Europe's wishes, the Ottoman Empire changed direction during his reign.

Bayezid II

Mehmed II died in Gebze at the age of 52. After 28 years as a sultan, he had defeated two empires and conquered 14 states and over 200 cities.

Pax Ottomana

Regardless of whether Bayezid poisoned his father, his reign started with the kind of chaos that could be expected after such a sudden takeover. As had more or less become the norm by now, his first battles were against a brother in pursuit of the throne. Cem, his brother, made successful attacks on Bursa, Inegöl, and later, Ankara, Anatolia, and Konya, though he only managed to rule them for a short time. Bayezid defeated his brother with the support of his father's armies, and Cem first fled to the Knights Hospitaller on Rhodes and later to mainland Italy under the Pope's protection. What Cem didn't know was that his brother had bribed the Christian rulers to continue holding him as a prisoner. Cem was not a guest but a hostage in Italy, and he died in prison in Neapel while Bayezid unified and amalgamated the territories his father had annexed.

As a ruler, Bayezid's emphasis was to keep the empire together, to coalesce and strengthen the state apparatus, and integrate minorities with the same incentives as his father. Except for a military campaign that resulted in full control over the Peloponnese and some minor battles with the Shah of Iran in the east, Bayezid did not take to expanding the empire further by conquest. He is most remembered for the evacuation of Jewish and Muslim populations persecuted by the Inquisition in the newly formed Spain. His action bears witness as to the high level of tolerance in the Ottoman Empire, where they not only welcomed refugees but helped them to escape. The cruelty of the Spanish Inquisition stands out in clear contrast to the millet policies which guaranteed a certain level of religious freedom. Bayezid sent his trusted vizier with an Ottoman fleet to ensconce religious minorities in the Ottoman territories. Bayezid is said to have laughed at the stupidity of Ferdinand and Isabella of Spain for "impoverishing their own country and enriching mine!" The Jewish minority was seen as an asset, useful both culturally and economically, and Bayezid encouraged his subjugates to welcome the refugees with open arms. He became known as "Bayezid the Just", and his reign was the beginning of what historians today call the Pax Ottomana—a reference to the Pax Romana, which was a period of peace and prosperity in the earlier Roman Empire. Historians using the term Pax Ottomana refer to the time of Bayezid and the two following emperors, who also shared the goal of developing laws and regulations, giving people freedom and responsibilities as citizens, strengthening the authoritarian rule of the sultan, and building strong relationships of trust between the sultan, viziers, officials, judges, the military, and people. The work had been initiated by Mehmed II, and his successors realized the benefits of building a state based on liberation rather than subjugation, thus gaining respect and dedication in all lines. Apart from the development of political institutions, Bayezid II shared the same interest in culture, religion, science, and education as his father, and the court looked upon other cultures as an opportunity to learn and share.

With the takeover of Crimea and Peloponnesus, the Ottomans also came to dominate trade on the Mediterranean and the Black Sea. In the perfect location to be the only gateway between Europe and Asia, the Ottoman Empire became a natural melting pot, which greatly benefited both the rulers and the people living under the empire.

Bayezid II was also notable for his many children as a result of his eight marriages. Not only did he have 8 sons but also 12 daughters, who were married off in politically convenient arrangements with families all around the empire. As Bayezid grew older, his sons became hungry for power and coveted the throne. Even before he was dead, civil war broke out in 1509 between Ahmet and Selim, two of his sons. Ahmet gathered an unexpected army and succeeded in conquering Karamanid, as well as fighting back a Safavid uproar in Asia Minor. Bolstered by the success, he turned toward Constantinople, where his aging father refused to let him in. In his place, Selim found support among the Janissaries and defeated and killed Ahmet in battle. Selim then, more or less, forced his father to abdicate at the age of 62. Bayezid II withdrew to retire in the territory where he'd been born. Just as mysterious and sudden as his father had, Bayezid died on the road, possibly poisoned by the newly-acclaimed emperor.

Selim I

Selim started his reign by executing his other brothers and chased his nephew, Ahmet's son, into exile. Selim's rule was short but efficient and is generally considered a break in the Pax Ottomana. One cause for Selim's more bellicose persona in comparison to both his father and his future heir was a rising threat in the east; after several decades of relative peace and internal stability, the Sunni Ottoman Muslims discovered a new enemy in the Shiite Persians. Persian Shah Ismail was on a quest to spread Shia Islam all throughout Eurasia, Asia Minor, and across the border into Anatolia. This was the beginning of an ongoing antagonism between Shia and Sunni Islam, thanks to a mutual, personal derision between Selim and Shah Ismail, who sent messages containing insults back and forth while marching into battle with each other. Selim had also put a very strict embargo on Persian silk by shutting Persia's borders, intending to close Ismail off from the rest of the world's trade. While marching on Persia, Selim was treated to scorched earth tactics as Ismail drew further back into his kingdom, trying to starve the Ottoman armies. He was also fighting the Uzbek in the Far East, and his applicable forces were fewer than the large army coming from the west. When they caught up in Chaldiran in August 1514 after only two years of Selim's rule, the Turks were weakened but still outnumbered the Safavids under Ismail's rule.

The battle was swift and acutely executed. What made the victory even more decisive was access to artillery, something the Ottomans had acquired under Mehmed II that the Persian Shah repeatedly had refused to do. Selim gained large amounts of land in northern Iraq, northwestern Iran, and present-day Azerbaijan, while the influence of the Shah diminished. He withdrew to his palace, never to be seen on a battlefield again.

After this success, Selim went on to complete his grandfather's dreams of conquering Egypt, currently under the rule of the Mamluks, where, in Cairo, the last Abbasid Caliph sat on the throne. Again, the Ottomans were faced with a traditionally equipped enemy army, proud to use bow and arrow instead of modernizing their armaments. Against the skilled Janissaries equipped with modern firearms and arquebuses, they didn't stand much of a chance, and Syria was conquered in a single battle. Shortly thereafter, Egypt was defeated after two quick battles, and the Caliph was exiled to Constantinople.

At that time, Selim was in possession of Damascus, Cairo, and Jerusalem, causing the Arabian Peninsula to fear that he was coming for Mecca and Medina. The Sharif of Mecca submitted to Selim without a fight, and with that the holiest cities of Islam had fallen into his hands easier than could have been anticipated. This was a significant conquest, as it shifted the center of the empire from the old Byzantine past toward important, Arabic Islamic strongholds. Selim was graced with the humble title of "The Servant of the Two Holy Cities", and today it is debated whether or not the exiled Caliph transferred his title to Selim, as historians from the 17th century had claimed. Since Selim did not exercise any sacred rights following his possible elevation, modern historians conclude this was not the case.

Selim's reign lasted only eight years, but his legacy was of great importance to what would come with Suleiman, the next ruler. The eight years of conquest expanded the area of the Ottoman Empire by 70%, an expansion made possible thanks to Selim's father and grandfather's interest in science and modernisation. The acquisition of superior armaments and weapons proved pivotal in battles with the traditionally equipped Safavid and Mamluk armies, whereas the modernisation of the Ottoman armies had started since the conquest of Constantinople under the lead of Mehmed II some 60 years earlier. The Janissaries had developed into a very strong and forceful nucleus, which played a major part in Selim's successful conquests. Together with the fiscal and political apparatus improved under Bayezid II, the Ottoman Empire became a world force, ready to take the lead in political, economic, cultural, and military arenas in and outside their territory. All of this paved the way for the real apogee of the Ottoman Empire under the rule of Selim's successor, Suleiman the Magnificent.

Selim I died after only eight years as a sultan, and though his legacy includes great territorial conquests, little is known about him as a ruler. It is also unclear as to how and why he died, though the records suggest a few different possibilities. Some say he died of a plague raging in the area, while other sources state he died of cancer or a skin disease called Sirpence. There are also suspicions his physician might have poisoned him, which is not unlikely considering Selim's somewhat grim reputation. He had a bad habit of executing his viziers, resulting in the coining of the curse popular at the time: "May you be a vizier of Selim's."

However he died, be it an act of revenge or natural causes, his successor ascended the throne surprisingly peacefully. Though his heir, Suleiman, had many brothers, none of them are mentioned in contemporaneous records, suggesting it might have been evident from childhood that the intelligent, eloquent, benevolent, and prudent Suleiman would shoulder his father's responsibilities when the day came. Suleiman was 27 at the time of his father's death, mature enough to revive the Pax Ottomana within his empire.

Suleiman the Magnificent

By the time of Suleiman's ascension, the Ottoman Empire was already in good condition. It was politically stable, culturally flourishing, dominating trade in the area, and in possession of a superior military organisation, which allowed Suleiman I to continue his predecessors' work without much need to change the direction of the empire. Selim's aggressive rule left the Janissaries efficient and strong, the Mamluks defeated, and the holy cities subsumed into the empire. The Republic of Venice in the west, as well as the Safavids in the east, had been weakened, and for the first time, the Ottoman had a fleet able to challenge old trade structures and rise as a new dominant power on the seas. Things were going well, and Suleiman intended to keep it that way.

During his childhood, he studied history, science, literature, theology, and military tactics at the Topkapi Palace in Istanbul. While living in the palace, he became very close friends with Pargali Ibrahim, one of the slave boys who later became vizier and was one of Suleiman's most trusted friends. Suleiman spoke no less than six languages and wrote poetry in three of them. His intellectual capabilities became evident later in life when he rewrote and organised the Kanuni, the laws concerning fiscal and economic issues, and instituted the judicial practices of millets, making ruling the empire more efficient. Suleiman also had a fascination for Alexander the Great, and after reading several biographies on the Macedonian King, he emulated Alexander's military strategies in his various campaigns. Under his father and grandfather's reigns, Suleiman had ruled a province in Crimea in preparation for becoming sultan.

While his somewhat belligerent father had been shaped by his fiery temperament and harsh judgment, Suleiman was more prudent and of a calmer and more pragmatic mind. One of his first actions as sultan was to lift the embargo on the silk trade to and from Persia, which had hurt Turkish traders as much as the Safavids. He then instituted a tax on all citizens, which meant that no matter what a person's ranking or standing was, they would still be subject to taxes. Instead of the whimsical exceptions for people of certain families or descent, the new, transparent tax system would have everyone pay taxes according to their income, a system still largely used today. He later instituted protections for Christians and Jews, freeing them from serfdom and giving the millets authority to rule their subjects according to their religion. Historians called Suleiman "the Magnificent", but to his contemporaries, he became known as "the Lawgiver".

Suleiman had expansionist dreams—not unlike any other Ottoman sultan—and he was immediately thrown into action when an uprising started in Damascus in 1521. Suleiman personally went to fight his first battle as sultan and won quite easily when the treacherous, Ottoman-appointed governor was killed in the same battle. Later that year, Suleiman rode west aiming for Belgrade, one of the last Christian strongholds in Ottoman territory, under the rule of the Hungarian Kingdom at the time. By using both infantry, cavalry, and heavy siege armaments from land as well as a flotilla of ships hindering potential aid arriving via the Danube, Belgrade's futile attempts to defend itself were of little use, and the city fell in less than two months.

The Ottoman expansion continued targeting Christians, as had been the habit for many hundreds of years. Though the founders of the Ottoman Empire—Osman and his first successor, Orhan—had not been strong advocates of the Islamic faith, religion was an integral part of both private and official life in the empire. In the 16th century, it had become such a strong, defining element that most campaigns led by Ottoman sultans were religious in nature, whether against the old Christian enemies or the new Shiite Muslim opponents in the east. Because of this, Suleiman was compelled to march south toward Rhodes to expel the Knight Hospitallers who had resided on the island since the time of the Crusades. The knights had become a nuisance to many groups of surrounding Muslims of late, mostly through acts of piracy. The knights captured ships from the Ottomans and other Muslim states, stealing valuable goods and cargo and enslaving the Muslim crews. They also attacked Muslim ships passing by on their way to perform Hajj, the Muslim pilgrimage, in Mecca. This was something Selim had failed to put to an end during his reign and which Suleiman made his priority.

The residing knights had already anticipated an attack from the Ottomans and had been fortifying their capital using Muslim slaves as labor. By the time of the siege of Rhodes, the capital of the island had three rings of stone walls as protection and the knights were prepared for the vengeful Ottomans heading their way. Starting with a fleet of 400 ships followed by an army of 100,000 men led by Suleiman himself, the siege started in June 1522. The fortifications resisted the fury of Ottoman bombings and gunpowder mines, and the inhabitants of Rhodes refused to acquiesce to Suleiman. After months of waves of invigorating progress followed by demoralising setbacks, both sides were exhausted. No other Christian allies had come to aid the Knights Hospitallers when the Ottomans had a slight upper-hand in the internecine siege. Through major losses, it was just a matter of time before the walls would eventually give in.

A medieval depiction of Turkish Janissaries laying siege to Rhodes

A truce was negotiated in November, but the population's demands for safety and privileges were too high for Suleiman to accept. The siege continued for another month until the civilians had finally had enough and pressured the knights' Grand Master to negotiate peace. Suleiman showed no acrimony and gave the knights—as well as the civil population—generous terms. The knights were given 12 days to leave and allowed to take weapons, personal belongings, and any religious relics they wanted along with them. The population was given the possibility to live under Ottoman rule for three years and were able to leave whenever they wanted during this trial period. The people who chose to permanently settle on the island would be free of taxes for five years and guaranteed freedom of religion under the promise that no churches would be desecrated and turned into mosques. Most of the population stayed on the island, now a part of the Ottoman Empire. The knights marched from the city in January of the following year onto Suleiman's ships heading for Crete. He had chosen not to annihilate the Knights Hospitaller—something many of his predecessors might have done—after the successful siege. His aim had been to control trade in the Mediterranean, a goal he achieved in the name of Islam. Instead of instigating fear and hatred, his prudent nature and diplomatic solutions earned him respect across Europe and Central Asia, which was uncommon for a conqueror of his measures.

After Rhodes, he resumed his European campaign, which was preceded by some remarkable circumstances. The Habsburg Dynasty had taken over the lead of the Holy Roman Empire, currently under the rule of Charles V, one of the strongest rulers in medieval and Renaissance

Europe. Charles V had chosen to battle the Franks, imprisoning their king after he ceded significant land to the Holy Roman Empire. Now, French King Francis I turned to Suleiman to form an unholy alliance against the Habsburg Empire, an alliance that greatly shocked and offended the Christian world. As it turned out, it was an alliance that would last over three centuries.

Charles V

Francis I

Francis asked Suleiman to wage war on the Habsburgs, residing in Vienna, which coincided with Suleiman's aim to conquer Hungary. Suleiman made Hungary the first stop on the road to Vienna, with the Battle of Mohács taking place just outside of Buda, the capital of the Hungarian kingdom. The Hungarian army suffered from the same shortcomings as many of the Ottomans' other defeated enemies - their army had not acquired modern armaments, but they still invited the enemy to fight in an open field. The Hungarian army had the opportunity to strike the Ottomans in a weakened state after they had marched in the scorching heat for days, but this would not have been considered chivalrous, so the two met in battle after the Ottomans were allowed some rest. Not only did the Ottomans heavily outnumber the Hungarian forces, but they also had about four times as many guns and more than three times as many cannons. The Battle of Mohács could have only ended in one way, and after a few hours, the Hungarians had suffered massive losses, incurring about 20,000 casualties while the Ottomans had lost about 1,500. The king of Hungary, Louis II, escaped at nightfall but fell off his horse and drowned in a river nearby. Most of his army were either annihilated or captured and by the end of the battle,

Suleiman was left shaking his head in disbelief, wondering how the great Hungarian kingdom had only been able to muster a tiny, suicidal force to meet them. As a precaution, the Ottomans waited several days before entering Buda, expecting retribution by a second army. When it didn't appear, they walked into the capital, and the once mighty Hungary saw its last traces of freedom for many centuries to come.

An Ottoman depiction of the battle

Louis II

The losses for the Hungarians include men and territory, but the Battle of Mohács became a watershed in Hungary's history. Over a span of 400 years, old Hungary would be occupied by Ottomans, the Holy Roman Empire, the Austrian Empire, and the Soviet Union, until they finally regained their autonomy in 1989, albeit in an incapacitated state. All this was unknown to Suleiman in 1526 as he recuperated in the capital, initiating a plan to besiege Vienna.

Different chroniclers analyze Suleiman's behavior in different ways. There is a plethora of opinions as to his motives for attempting the takeover of Vienna, a well-guarded city far away from his empire's center. Had he intended to conquer the whole of the Holy Roman Empire? Had he intended to strengthen his borders? Had he acted in accordance with King Francis I's needs in the West? No matter the reason, Suleiman did not halt in his advances, despite the fact circumstances were not favorable for the Ottomans. The summer rains had already begun when he set out for Vienna, making most of the roads inaccessible both for cavalry and moving the heavy pieces of artillery needed for a successful siege. The camels brought from Anatolia proved too sensitive for the cold, constant rain and died in large numbers, and many of the soldiers shared the same fate.

By the time they arrived around Vienna in late September, the Ottoman forces were heavily depleted, and many siege armaments had been left behind when stuck in the mud. The population of Vienna had seen the enemy coming, giving them plenty of time to reinforce, strengthen, and prepare. When they launched the siege, the Ottoman forces lacked conviction, making it easy to fight back during the initial attacks. After making no real progress, the soldiers lost their motivation when the weather took a turn for the worse shortly into the siege. Suleiman's supply of food and water diminished, and the troops were close to mutiny. In a final "all or nothing" attempt, the Ottomans attacked with all the strength they had left, trying to break Vienna's fortifications, which refused to yield. Suleiman accepted defeat, gathered his men, and returned to Anatolia. The hasty departure from Vienna resulted in the loss of heavy armaments, as well as troops and prisoners in the heavy snowfall.

Modern historians speculate as to why Suleiman persisted with the siege even though the Ottoman forces were evidently weaker than the forces in Vienna upon their arrival. As an experienced, strategic warrior, it is most likely he realized his disadvantage and the full scale of his potential losses. It was also probable that the last burst of attacks was merely a means with which to weaken the city walls for a future siege. The second attempt, in 1532, was met with the same mix of bad luck and good defenses, and Vienna marked the limit of Ottoman advances in the West. Suleiman had to turn back to his homeland to face his Shiite antagonist in the east, the new Safavid Shah of Persia Tahmasp.

Shah Tahmasp deposed and executed the Ottoman governor of Baghdad in 1532, and one of the vassal states under Ottoman rule in eastern Anatolia switched sides, swearing allegiance to the shah. In response, Suleiman sent his trusted friend and grand vizier Ibrahim Pasha to initiate the fighting, with the emperor himself showing up the following year. While the Ottomans were marching towards an anticipated battle, Tahmasp employed the same tactics as his predecessor, burning the terrain and withdrawing into his own territories. This pattern repeated itself three times in the coming 20 years, and Suleiman never actually fought Tahmasp in battle. In the wake of an outright war, he annexed the deserted territories in southern Georgia and Azerbaijan, northern and western Iraq, and some of the coastlines of the Persian Gulf. The two parties signed a peace treaty in 1554.

While the landmasses remained stable under Suleiman's rule, real progress was made on the open waters. The Ottoman fleet quickly became a dominating force, and when Suleiman feared a challenge from the Spanish Armada, he employed the notorious Hayreddin Barbarossa Pasha to command his fleet. Under his command, the Ottoman fleet expanded their influence in the Mediterranean, taking the North African coastline where Tunisia, Morocco, and Algeria had become autonomous provinces. He later captured Nice and pillaged the Italian west coast. This affirmed Ottoman dominance in the Eastern Mediterranean. Somalia, Africa's Horn, Yemen, and present-day Oman were also conquered by the Ottomans. They also conducted trade with Mughal India and helped relieve the Sultanate of Aceh from Portuguese raids as far away as

Sumatra.

Hayreddin Barbarossa Pasha

Suleiman had, with help from his capable and trusted officers, expanded the empire to reach farther than ever before, keeping his borders safe and lands in order all the while. His failure to capture Vienna stands out in a long list of successful battles, but he is still remembered more as the "lawgiver" than a warlord.

The Kanun was an earthly code of laws used as a complement to Sharia, the divine law, in matters the Sharia did not entertain. To write the Kanun, Suleiman took to collecting and reading all of the legislative decisions his nine predecessors had taken, analysing and comparing them carefully, before using them as the foundation for the new set of laws. The job took many years, but once it was done, the Kanun and the Sharia were used as the code of laws for the next 300 years in the Ottoman Empire.

Suleiman's most important changes were the inclusion of Christian and Jewish minorities, who were lifted from serfdom. This prompted Christians from other parts of the world to migrate to the Ottoman Empire to live a better life under Suleiman's rule.

He was also known for instituting a great number of schools for younger and older boys. The mosques he built often had a school within the compound, giving Muslim boys the opportunity to learn what he had learned as a young boy. Suleiman was also a patron of the arts and gathered no less than 600 artists of various backgrounds and nationalities in his Ehl-i Hiref Community of the Craftsmen. Many of them were poets—as was Suleiman himself—who wrote some of the most memorable lines in both Persian and Turkish. Many of his verses and proverbs are still frequently quoted.

Another one of his lasting legacies was the remodelling of Constantinople itself. He was, by and large, the main renovator of the city, and together with renowned architect Mimar Sinan, he built bridges, palaces, official buildings, and mosques. He even took to restoring the Dome of the Rock in Jerusalem; the walls surrounding old Jerusalem today are also Mimar Siman's work, paid for by the sultan. The Kaaba in Mecca was renovated by the duo as well.

To successfully succeed as a man of so many talents after a flourishing golden age lasing more than 45 years, it would take more than an ordinary leader. Suleiman had outlived two of his sons but still had four more who claimed to be the right person for the job. Though he had written a full code of laws, there was still no set order of succession. The only mandatory rule concerning the transmission of power was the practice of fratricide instituted by Mehmed II in an effort to prevent any uprisings once the new sultan had been installed, and since the empire was at its height, competition for the throne would be fiercer than before.

Not only did the brothers get involved, but Suleiman's second wife, Hürrem Sultan, played a vital role in conspiring with her sons. Hürrem Sultan was a woman of great influence, simply because Suleiman was head over heels in love with her. His first wife had been put aside, and Hürrem, a slave girl from the harem, rose to become the sultan's favorite and wife, to the astonishment of many. Suleiman had intended his first son by his first wife, Mustafa—a very accomplished warrior and intellectual—to inherit the throne. In contrast, Hürrem, had wanted one of her sons to take the throne to avoid the risk of execution for either of them. Though Mustafa had been favored by Suleiman, the people, the court, and Suleiman's friend, Grand Vizier Ibrahim Pasha, Hürrem managed to convince her husband to have Mustafa executed and Ibrahim Pasha accused treason. The stories about the rounds of executions—among them his first-born son, his grand vizier, his finance secretary Iskender Celebi, his other son Bayezid, and four grandsons—with which Suleiman ended his reign are as many as the victims. Of his two remaining sons, one is said to have died of grief. Suleiman had six sons, yet there was only one left at the time of his death.

The Era of Transformation

Old Suleiman died as a great warlord should, out campaigning in Hungary just before a victory was proclaimed for the Ottoman forces. He was nearly 72 years old and died of old age, rather than due to poison or conspiracy. Suleiman died in 1566, leaving his power in the hands of Selim II.

Selim II

Surprisingly, after all the turmoil and commotion, Selim showed very little interest in ruling the sultanate, leaving most of the decision making in the hands of his grand vizier, Sokollu Mehmed. Sokollu Mehmed managed to strike a deal with the Habsburgs to ensure Ottoman access to Moldavia and Wallachia, as well as the donation of a yearly gift to the Ottoman Empire as a token of peace. Selim II was the first sultan who never went on campaign, and Sokollu Mehmed was the one to wage war as far north as Astrakhan and as far south as Yemen. Northern ambitions were held back by the Russian Tsar, and after some initial success and the conquering of Cyprus, the Ottoman fleet met resistance and was defeated by the Spanish and Italian navies at the Battle of Lepanto. At that time, Spanish and Portuguese kings and queens initiated the colonial period which led to internal issues for the Ottoman Empire. Selim II's reign was short-lived and in no way comparable to his father's, but when he died, he was remembered as a calm and good person, not as one who stood out by having lived an excessive lifestyle. His grand vizier lived on to serve the next sultan in line, Murad III.

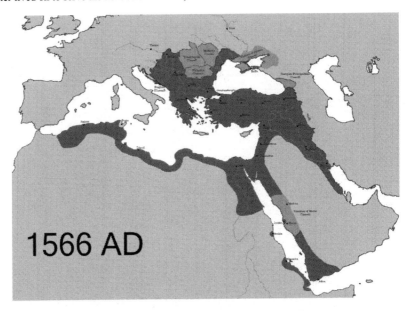

A map of the Ottoman Empire at the time of Suleiman's death

Murad III

The time after Suleiman's death was once recognised by scholars and historians as the "Decline of the Ottoman Empire," but this consensus opinion changed in the 1980s and is now commonly referred to as the "Era of Transformation." The following years were not necessarily a decline but a shift in the empire's focus, where the constant expansion and warring halted in exchange for internal stability. The focus would necessarily shift to maintaining the status quo as one of the world's leading empires, a difficult quest when the Habsburg takeover of the Holy Roman Empire and the beginning of the colonial period as initiated by Spain and Portugal are taken into consideration. Another issue was the necessity to replace the mandatory fratricide instituted by Mehmed II. Suleiman's frenzy of executions had proven that even a just and sophisticated ruler could resort to emotional outbursts with dire consequences. Selim II only had had one wife but had managed to produce no less than seven sons, so Murad III had five of his brothers strangled.

His reign was defined by significant factors initiating the transformation of the Ottoman Empire. Firstly, he followed in his father's footsteps by never heading out on campaign himself.

It was still the highly competent Grand Vizier Sokollu Mehmed who had led the armies into battles when Murad thought it necessary. Murad reigned for two decades during which he never left Constantinople, making him quite unpopular in the writings of contemporaneous historians.

Grand Vizier Sokollu Mehmed Pasha

Another significant factor was the rapid population growth. During the 16th century, the empire experienced an influx of people to the empire due to political reforms considered beneficial for all classes of citizens, but also due to good farming conditions and trade. At the end of the century, the population had actually grown too large for the available resources and many peasants had to give up farming due to the lack of land. They took to pillaging and plundering in bandit-style gangs instead, becoming a destabilizing political issue in Anatolia. Another agitator was the increase of precious metals in West Europe after various colonial conquests. Silver and gold arrived in great quantities, causing an inflation in both southern Europe and the Ottoman Empire. This led the previously stable and controlled economy to face the challenges of a rising population and economic decline simultaneously. To further fuel the flame, the inflation led to dissatisfaction within the Janissaries corps, and their set salaries decreased in value among higher government officials. The last factor was that as a result of Murad spending all of his time in his capital, the people around him at the court were more influenced by his decisions than the provincial officials, his campaigning grand vizier, or his other officers who were out fighting. He based his opinions more and more on the people personally and emotionally related to him than on the skilled officials he had employed to advise him professionally. In the same vein, Suleiman I had been the first sultan to elevate a slave from the harem to become his wife, which opened up the opportunity for more women to make their way into the inner circles of power. Instead of marriage by lineage or dynasty, women of all castes could find a way to rise to power, just like the men in government positions. This led to women in harems—as well as the sultan's mother, sister, and wife—having an increased influence. The period, which lasted until the end of the 17th century—is sometimes referred to as the Sultanate of Women, due to the fact that many of the rulers were minors. Various women became prominent figures with the legal right to interfere in the empire's political affairs. Murad III's mother, Nurban, is known as one of the most powerful mother sultans, famous for having plotted with his sister against his strong, decisive wife sultan, Safiye. Their influence led to many entanglements at the court, and Murad subsequently ending up having more children than any of his predecessors. Rumors at the time counted his offspring at nearly 100, though this number may be somewhat exaggerated.

Either way, the internal commotion was, in many ways, more severe than the wars raging on the eastern and western fronts of the empire. Murad III had decided to take advantage of the death of Persian Shah Tahmasp and unravel the 1555 peace treaty, an act which Grand Vizier Sokollu Mehmed opposed. Though he was, in fact, the one in charge of the empire's military campaigns and had been for nearly 15 years, his opinion was ignored, and the Ottoman-Safavid war broke out in 1577. It would be 12 years before peace could be negotiated, and with great gains for the Ottomans. Murad had expressed some jealousy of the grand vizier's popularity, and shortly after the war had broken out, Sokollu Mehmed was allegedly assassinated by an agent acting on the order of Mehmed's wife, Safiye. With this murder, Safiye had removed a big obstacle to her influence over both her husband and her sons, the next generation of sultans.

Once peace had been negotiated with the Safavids, the Ottomans turned west and initiated what became known as the Long War with the Habsburgs, which was to continue after Murad's death and into the next century under Mehmed III, the next ruler.

Except for the long war, Mehmed III is mostly remembered for having executed no less than 19 of his brothers and half-brothers while rising to the throne. Mehmed chose to lead his armies in battle, which had not been done by a sultan since Suleiman I's reign. After one successful battle, in which it is said the sultan tried to flee halfway in, he returned to Constantinople, promising to lead more campaigns against the Habsburg Empire. His doctor, however, pronounced him as being in too poor health for further campaigns, due to his excessive eating and drinking. This was perhaps also in accordance with the sultan's own secret wishes. During his 8 year reign, the empire was mainly ruled by Safiye, his valide sultan. Mehmed III died at the age of 37. Some contemporaneous historians claim Mehmed died of distress after he had executed one of his ambitious sons (on Safiye's advice), and some claim he died of the plague or a stroke. Safiye had the legal rights to make all political decisions and was instrumental in deciding the faith of many prominent viziers, officials, and advisors.

Mehmed III

The succeeding sultan, Ahmed I, was first in line who did not practice the tradition of fratricide. He spared his only brother, Mustafa, while ascending to the throne. This was probably because Sultan Ahmed I was only 13 years old at that point and had not yet produced any heirs. If he were to die with no male family members to follow him, it would have endangered the dynasty. Mustafa and his grandmother, Safiye, were sent to the old palace in Bayezit to live far away from the intrigue in Constantinople. Though Safiye was, by then, the old valide sultan, Ahmed was well aware of her ambition and influence at the court and paid her a good amount in retirement money as motivation for her to stay out of Ottoman politics.

Ahmed I

When taking over power from his father, Ahmed had also inherited the war against the Habsburgs. By then, it had been raging for over a decade with very little success on either side, though they had both suffered detrimental losses. In the domestic territory of Anatolia, the Celali rebellions were coming to a climax and in need of resolution. On top of that, a new war had broken out with the Safavid Empire, under the rule of Shah Abbas I.

The long war with the Habsburgs ended in 1606 with the Peace of Zsitvatorok. The treaty, signed by both emperors, was negotiated to last 20 years and settled the borders that were more or less drawn in the same way they had been before the conflict broke out. This result demonstrated the Ottomans' inability to challenge the Habsburg Empire, and it would be another 80 years before war would break out again between the two.

This did not mean rest for Ahmed or his armies, as Abbas I in Persia had taken the opportunity to invade Ottoman territory while they were still fighting in the west. The Ottomans were unprepared for an attack from the east and had to rush to attempt their defense. The Safavids had finally modernized their army with the help of England, and reconquering their territory proved no difficulty.

The two armies met at the shore of Lake Urmia, where the Ottomans suffered a shattering defeat. With the death of the commander and the simultaneous uprisings in eastern Anatolia, the war with the Safavids was paused in favor of trying to settle the internal unrest. Constantinople saw its share of conflict, with the rising tension between the prestigious Janissary Elite Corps and the Sipahi, the upper cavalry composing their own social class. Young Ahmed sent his grand vizier, Murad Pasha, to fight the rebels in the east, with a strategy that later earned him the epithet "Kuyucu", or "Gravedigger". The tactics he employed consisted of rebels either joining the army as mercenaries or being slaughtered by it, which quickly and efficiently solved the issue of the uprisings. By 1610, Ahmed was able to start resettling villagers who had fled the chaos.

After the death of the grand vizier, the wars with Persia were slightly halted, and both sides proclaimed they were willing to negotiate peace and lay down their weapons. A treaty was signed, though it did not last for more than three years, and conflict broke out again and continued beyond Ahmed's death.

His political and cultural heritage went hand-in-hand with his religious nature, and his main legacy was the building of the Blue Mosque—the Sultan Ahmed Mosque as it is known today— in Istanbul. He had a love for poetry but an aversion to painting, stating it was sacrilege to depict living beings to rival Allah's perfect creation. He was also adamant when enforcing attendance at Friday prayer, banned the use of alcohol, and initiated the return to a more conservative religious culture. In addition, he transformed the tax system to support new recruitment to—and the expansion of—the armies, which had been depleted after the long war in the west. The taxes were unpopular, and the displeasure of the Janissaries would continue to be a nuisance for Ahmed's successors in the years to come.

The Blue Mosque

Dying in 1617 from typhus, the 27-year-old Ahmed was the first sultan who was not succeeded by a son but by his brother, Mustafa. It was also the first time a sultan had been appointed by age rather than linage, however, it quickly became evident that Mustafa I was not mentally stable, and he was deposed within his first year of rule. In 1618, Ahmed's 13-year-old son, Osman, took the throne, full of enthusiasm and hoping to restore the sultan's authority over the other, powerful institutions within the empire. First, after enormous losses on the way to Ardabil, he managed to agree to a peace treaty with the Safavids in the east. Once there, the Ottomans gained control over the conflict, and this time, the signed treaty lasted. Empowered by the success, he took to personally leading his armies in an attempt to invade Poland in the autumn of 1621. This ended in a disappointing stalemate between the two, and the Ottomans returned home with no gains to show. Osman II blamed the failure on the Janissaries' low morale and cowardice, and he initiated plans to build another army from the former rebels who were now mercenaries in the east to replace the Janissaries.

Mustafa I

Osman II

The Janissaries had, by then, become a powerful social class in their own right, and their loyalty toward the sultan had waned through the decades. Their social ambitions were often aired in the coffeehouses around the capital, where they gathered to plan their increase in power. Osman went on to close all coffeehouses to prevent them from sedition, an act leading to resentment within the Janissaries and the Sipahi. The fact that Osman's mother had died a few years prior had cost him a great deal of support from the court, and without a valide sultan, his reign was rapidly coming to an end.

The Janissaries revolted with the sanction of the court, and for the first time in Ottoman history, a reigning sultan was overthrown and murdered. This signaled the end of the patrimonial empire and the sovereignty of the sultan in favor of the shared power between different institutions of authority.

The 17-year-old Osman's death led to a reinstatement of his uncle, Mustafa, but only for a short year. After being deposed for a second time, he was replaced with another of his brother's sons, Murad IV, who was merely 11 years old at the time. Because of the sultan's young age, the empire was ruled mainly by his mother, Valide Sultan Kösem Sultan. In all parts of the empire, unrest was once again rising, and many groups worked together for independence, increased power, or overthrowing the ruling dynasty. The Janissaries in the capital stormed the palace in an uprising, killing the grand vizier of Murad, who, in turn, had his brother's regicide fresh in mind. He decided to reinstate his power as sultan to create order in the broken lines of his subordinates.

Murad IV

Among his reforms was a military land tenure to strengthen the army. He also encouraged peasants to farm abandoned fields, and he banned all consumption of alcohol, tobacco, and coffee in the capital itself, making their use punishable by death. It is even said he went out at night dressed as a civilian to patrol the streets and personally enforce his new laws, executing those breaking them on the spot.

The only military campaign he carried out was the final war with the Safavids, which ended in the Ottomans' favor, settling the borders as they had previously been decided in the Peace of Amasya in 1555. The borders set at that point are still more or less the same today, now separating Iran, Iraq, and Turkey.

By the end of Murad's reign, the empire was slightly more stable than when he had ascended the throne, but unfortunate circumstances had deprived him of his 10 sons before they had even reached puberty. When Murad IV died at the age of 27 from cirrhosis, the only option for a sultan of Ottoman origin was Ahmed I and Kösem Sultan's last remaining son, Ibrahim. During his brother's years at the throne, Ibrahim had been held in what was called the Kafes, a form of house arrest, confining the brothers of a sultan as a substitute to the previously mandatory practice of fratricide. In the Kafes, the brothers could be controlled, and potential plotting against the emperor could be monitored and curtailed. This, unfortunately, led to mental health issues for Ibrahim, which manifested as severe headaches and untimely collapses. During his rule of eight years, much of the work was done by his competent grand vizier, Kara Mustafa Pasha, a pattern which became common in the second half of the 17th century. Ibrahim had candor and was humble where Mustafa Pasha's knowledge was concerned. Ibrahim's bad health impacted his ability to perform as a sultan, and consequently, it was Mustafa Pasha who pushed for coinage reform, a new land-survey, a decrease in the size of the Janissaries, and efforts to get rid of non-contributing members of the state on the payroll. Meanwhile, Ibrahim's mother, Kösem Sultan, encouraged him to use the harem girls to distract him from his pain, as well as to produce heirs to the dynasty.

The distractions didn't play out entirely to Kösem Sultan's advantage—after a period of increased power when Ibrahim spent more and more time with the harem, she gained influence at the court, but he soon fell under the spell of the avaricious harem girls. Kösem Sultan was sent away to retire, and Ibrahim adhered more and more to a person who claimed to be a doctor, Cinci Hoca, who said he could cure Ibrahim's diseases. The ingratiating quack cajoled Ibrahim into executing his grand vizier and replacing him with one of Hoca's friends.

As Ibrahim's mind deteriorated and he lost connection with the outside world, he made unwelcome and costly decisions, promoting eight of his consorts and giving them all luxurious homes, riches, and lands. To his wife, a former harem girl, he clad a whole palace in sable furs.

His reign came to an abrupt end after he proclaimed war against the Venetians. The war mainly took place on the eastern Mediterranean and was not to the Ottomans' advantage. The Venetian fleet managed to blockade the Dardanelles, leading to a shortage of food and supplies in Constantinople. Ibrahim also raised taxes to compensate for his extravagant lifestyle and wartime spending, making him unpopular with the citizens as well as the Janissaries.

Ibrahim

After a revolt by the elite corps, Ibrahim was placed under house arrest and later executed, with his mother's consent. His successor was the young Mehmed IV, then only 7-years-old, and consequently, the old valide sultan, Kösem, backed by her Janissary allies, regained her power at the court. The following year, Kösem Sultan and the new grand vizier finally defeated and expelled the Venetians from the Dardanelles. The war raged on and along with palace intrigue, Mehmed's first years as sultan were also exacerbated by uprisings in the east. After his grandmother plotted to poison him, she was executed, and his own mother became valide sultan. In 1656, she appointed Köprülü Mehmed Pasha as grand vizier with full executive powers. The sultan was still only 14-years-old, but he had already been on the throne for seven years.

Köprülü Mehmed Pasha initiated a new era in which the Köprülü family held the grand vizier title for nearly 50 years, which helped stabilize the shaky territories. The Köprülü era started with a large number of executions of soldiers and officials considered disloyal to the Ottoman Dynasty, and Mehmed Pasha had to fight fiercely to establish his authority. He remained successful, and with the full support of Sultan Mehmed, he regained control of the military and was able to initiate some economic reform. Mehmed Pasha died of natural causes after five years as a grand vizier, and for the first time in Ottoman history, the title was inherited by an eldest son.

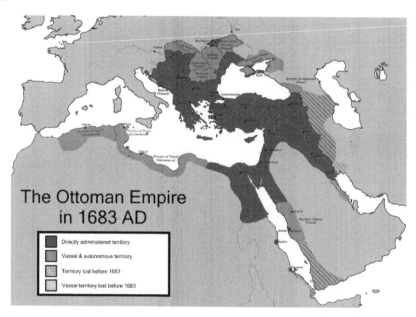

A map of the Ottoman Empire at its largest extent

The War of the Holy League

Mehmed IV is mainly remembered as "the Hunter", since this hobby took up much of his time. The competence of his grand viziers did not, however, render him passive, and though they managed much of the political affairs, he rode with his armies in battles all across Europe, not as a commander but a participant. It was the son of Mehmed Pasha, Fazil Ahmed, who led the armies in great campaigns across Europe, extending the empire's European territories further than ever before. He defeated the Venetians and ended the Cretan War, reinserted authority in Transylvania, and conquered some territories in Poland and western Ukraine. In 1676, he died from alcohol-related illnesses, and his brother-in-law, Kara Mustafa Pasha, was next in the family to take the title. After his initial success to conquer more territory in Ukraine, he decided to follow in the footsteps of Suleiman the Magnificent and do what he had not been able to:

conquer Vienna. In 1682, Kara Mustafa Pasha marched toward the Habsburg capital, intending to claim the strategically important city on the Danube River.

The series of battles in Poland, the Ukraine, and Russia had all led up to the battle of Vienna, unraveling old alliances and creating new ones. The Ottomans thought they had an opportunity by backing up Orthodox and Protestant kings against the Catholics, and Kara Mustafa considered the timing perfect. After having convinced Mehmed IV it was time to strike, an army of 100,000 marched toward central Europe in late summer of 1682. War was declared in August of the same year, after conquering two minor fortresses and settling to wait out the winter.

However, while they waited out the winter, the Habsburg Empire had time to reach out for backup. German Count von Starhemberg was left with only 15 000 men to defend Vienna after some 80,000 inhabitants fled the city. When summer arrived and the Ottomans with it, the count was promised relief from both Poland and Venice.

The attackers arrived with a large number of men but only 19 cannons, and the defenders had the opposite: a few men but cannons numbering around 370 pieces. Thanks to the strong defences of the city, the struggling citizens and soldiers were able to hold out long enough for help to arrive. Vienna was on its knees when the Polish and additional imperial Habsburg troops finally crossed the Danube and came to its relief. At the same time, Kara Mustafa's allies - the Serbs, Wallachians, and the Crimean Khan - failed to fulfil their promises. In fact, whether they participated at all or merely stood by watching the Ottomans fight is still debated among historians.

Another problem for Kara Mustafa could have been that he wanted the city intact, and thus he did not order a full-scale attack. The siege could have ended quickly and successfully had Kara Mustafa been more belligerent in his attacks. When the battle finally broke out against the newly arrived troops, the Ottomans were still trying to break into Vienna, which eventually led to their forces being tied down between the Polish, German, and Austrian troops. It is still widely debated how many men the Ottomans lost, but 20,000 is the smallest number mentioned in contemporaneous sources, and the aftermath led to Kara Mustafa's execution by order of Mehmed IV.

A 17th century painting depicting the Battle of Vienna

After the fighting around Vienna, the Holy League was now determined to push the Ottomans out of the European heartlands. The Battle of Vienna had only been the trigger for what would be known as the Great Turkish Wars in European history books, and as the War of the Holy League to Turkish scholars. The Holy League consisted of Papal States under the rule of Pope Innocent XI, the Holy Roman Empire under Emperor Leopold, the Polish-Lithuanian Commonwealth, the Venetian Republic, and later, the Tsardom of Russia. The alliance formed after the triumphant defense of Vienna and lasted for the next 16 years, fighting against Ottoman forces in Central Europe and the Balkans.

The first years of the War of the Holy League were detrimental to the Ottomans, who suffererd defeat after defeat, most significantly at the second Battle of Mohács in 1687, which led to mutiny among the troops. The Janissaries and Sipahis returned to Istanbul, and Mehmed was deposed that same autumn in favor of his brother, Suleiman II. The Holy League waged war against the Ottomans on many fronts, with the Republic of Venice on the Mediterranean, the Habsburgs in Hungary pushing for the Balkans, and the Russians coming from the north. On some fronts, Suleiman II, together with the Fazil Mustafa Pasha, the latest grand vizier from the

Köprulu family, managed to win some defining battles, but they also suffered some serious defeats. A decade of warfare on different fronts had taken its toll on troop numbers.

The War of the Holy League reached a stalemate during Suleiman's reign, but when he died of ill health—followed by the death of the grand vizier shortly thereafter—their successors could not manage to resist anymore. The new sultan, Ahmed II, had spent nearly 43 years in the Kafes and was, in many ways, unsuited to shoulder responsibilities in the midst of war. His grand vizier also showed little knowledge or interest in leading the armies, and after a severe defeat at the Battle of Slankamen, the Holy League pressed on, forcing the Ottomans to cede large territories from their European domains.

Ahmed died after just four years on the throne and was succeeded by a representative of the next generation, Mehmed IV's son, Mustafa II. Mustafa was determined to take back the lost lands and was initially successful in his ambitions. Though the 13 years of war had depleted the Ottoman army, at this point, the war had become costly both economically and socially. During the third campaign led by Mustafa against the Habsburgs, he suffered defeat in Zenta, losing his grand vizier in the battle. This more or less settled the preconditions for a peace treaty.

In 1699, the Treaty of Karlowitz was signed, marking the end of the War of the Holy League and the end of the Era of Transformation for the Ottoman Empire. During the last years of the war, before the treaty had been signed, the empire had pushed through some fiscal reforms. The war had been costly, but the Köprülü grand viziers had been economically pragmatic during their rule. They had increased taxation on luxury goods and tobacco, reformed the Janissaries' payroll, and pushed through changes in *waqf* collection, land taxes, and other fiscal improvements. This all led to the Ottoman Empire entering the 18th century with the territorial loss of Hungary, but with an economic surplus.

The Köprülü era had somewhat replaced the Sultanate of Women, and by the turn of the century, Mustafa had withdrawn to Edirne, leaving the power in the hands of his executive grand vizier. This grand vizier was infamous for his corruption and creating agitation along military lines. The newly implemented tax reforms had not played out according to plan, and a big portion of the collected taxes ended up in the collectors' pockets. The absence of the sultan and the nepotism of the grand vizier, together with long overdue Janissary salaries, finally led to a revolt and the deposition of the sultan in what is known as the Edirne Event. In 1703, Mustafa II was replaced by his brother and died later that year at the age of 39. The next century would be marked by a decline in power of the sultans and an increased Janissary influence.

Between 1453 and 1703, Ottoman history was marked by waves of strong sultans followed by periods of decentralisation and instability. The reigns of Mehmed the Conqueror and Suleiman the Magnificent were incredibly successful, at least where the territorial expansion of the empire and the reformation and adaptation of the military and politics were concerned, and that period was marked by a consensus allowing the sultan to rule authoritatively, more or less unopposed by lower officials. However, with the growth of the empire, the authoritative sultan needed increased help from other administrative institutions, leaving room for avaricious governors, officials, and viziers to rise in the ranks. Newly formed institutions became more influential, and the Janissaries gained in power, as did the women in direct relation to the sultan. These changes in the structure of the formerly authoritarian sultanate took place mainly after the death of Suleiman I and truly marked a transformation for the Ottoman Empire. Coincidently, this period also saw many sultans die rather early from disease and plague, which resulted in the heirs rising to the throne when they were still too young to rule. This was a vital factor in the marginalization of the sultan, and during the 17th century, most important decisions were made by the executive grand vizier or the sultan's mother, the valide sultan. The devastating wars against the Holy League and the passivity of the last sultan of the century were the last straws, resulting in the Janissaries' uprising and their eventual taking over of power.

From that point on, the sultan needed recognition from the powerful Janissaries, and during the 18th century, several sultans would have their reigns both initiated and terminated by the elite corps' demands. With the transformation complete, the following century would find the Ottoman Empire still dealing with old enemies still nibbling at their borders and new threats rising on the horizon.

Online Resources

Other books about Middle East history by Charles River Editors

Other books about the Ottomans on Amazon

Bibliography

Babinger, Franz, *Mehmed the Conqueror and his time,* Princeton University Press, 1992.

Bonner, Michael, et al., *Islam in the Middle Ages,* Praeger Publishers, 2009.

Clot, André, *Suleiman the Magnificent,* Saqi Books, 2012.

Cleveland, William L, *A History of the Modern Middle East,* Westview Press, 2000.

Finkel, Caroline, Osman's Dream: The Story of the Ottoman Empire, 1300-1923, Basic Books, 2005.

Hathaway, Jane, The Arab Lands under Ottoman Rule, 1516-1800, Pearson Education Ltd, 2008.

Howard, Douglas A, A History of the Ottoman Empire, Cambridge University Press, 2017.

Judson, Pieter M, *The Habsburg Empire,* The Belknap Press, 2016.

Kafadar, Cemal, Between Two Worlds: The Construction of the Ottoman State, University of California Press, 1995.

Karlsson, Ingmar, *Turkiets historia,* Historiska media, 2015.

McKay, John P., et al., *A History of World Societies,* Bedford/St Martins, 2014.

Nationalencyklopedin, NE, 2009.

Peirce, Leslie, The Imperial Harem: Women and Sovereignty in the Ottoman Empire, Oxford University Press, 1993.

Tezcan, Baki, The Second Ottoman Empire: Political and Social Transformation in the Early Modern World, Cambridge University Press, 2010.

Uyar, Mesut & Edward J. Erickson, *A Military History of the Ottomans,* Praeger Publishers, 2009.

Free Books by Charles River Editors

We have brand new titles available for free most days of the week. To see which of our titles are currently free, click on this link.

Discounted Books by Charles River Editors

We have titles at a discount price of just 99 cents everyday. To see which of our titles are currently 99 cents, click on this link.

81165444R00029

Made in the USA
Middletown, DE
21 July 2018